GILLY CUBITT
AND JUDY WILLIAMS

SALADS

HAMLYN

Produced by New Leaf Productions, Ashford, Kent.

Photography by Mick Duff
Design by Jim Wire
Typeset by System Graphics Ltd., Folkestone
Series Editor: James M. Gibson

First published in 1987 by
Hamlyn Publishing
Bridge House, 69 London Road
Twickenham, Middlesex, England

Copyright © The Hamlyn Publishing Group Limited 1987

ISBN 0 600 327 019

Printed in Hong Kong

We would like to thank:
Rosenthal studio-line and Thomas China for the loan of
china, glassware and cutlery used throughout the book;
Florrie and Don for their hospitality.

CONTENTS

THE STUFF OF SALADS – LETTUCE

All sorts of vegetables are used in salads, but the simplest mixtures of all are those that are made up of leaves.

Quattro Stagione – the same sort of shape and texture as round lettuce, but with reddish brown edges to the leaves. Imported, available July to September.

Round lettuce – soft, flexible leaves and a delicate buttery taste. Available all year round. Look too for little Gem lettuce hearts.

Lollo rosso – looks like curly endive (see page 6) but leaves have reddish brown frilly edges. Has a slightly bitter taste. Imported, available July to September.

Webb's lettuce – large, frilly leaves
with a crisp texture and clean taste.
Available May to September.

Oak leaf lettuce – a floppy, loose-leafed
lettuce with reddish brown leaves that
resemble their namesake and have a
slightly bitter taste. Also known as
feuille de chêne lettuce.
Available July to October.

Iceberg – crisp, long-lasting,
tightly curled lettuce. To
separate the leaves without
tearing them, cut out the stalk
and core and hold upside down
under a running tap. The water
eases the leaves apart gently.
Available all year round.

Cos lettuce – long, sturdy leaves with
a crisp stalk and coarse texture.
Available all year round.

. . . AND OTHER LEAVES

Spinach – choose only young and tender leaves for salads. They are robust and tasty and stand up well to the addition of a hot salad dressing. Available all year round.

Radicchio – another member of the chicory family. It looks like a rather overblown purplish red Brussels sprout and has a slightly tough texture and a bittersweet flavour. Available all year round.

Dandelion leaves – pick your own small tender leaves. They have an astringent, bitter flavour. Available June to August.

Chicory – tightly packed heads of white and pale yellow leaves. They are crisp with a rather bitter flavour. Imported, available September to June.

Curly endive – a large sprawling head of long frilly leaves. It's green around the edges and yellow in the centre with a coarse texture and pleasant bitter flavour. Available all year round.

Chinese leaves – looks rather like a pale and tightly packed Cos lettuce but has a softer texture, like cabbage. Available all year round.

Watercress – dark, glossy leaves with crisp stalks and a strong peppery, slightly metallic taste. Available all year round.

Salad cress – sprouted rape seeds have taken over from the original 'mustard and cress' mixture. It has a delicious nutty flavour and makes a pretty garnish. Available all year round.

PLUS THE USUAL...

Tomatoes – lots of varieties are available. Choose home- or Channel Island-grown, or go for the tiny cherry tomatoes (about 20 to 450 g/1 lb). The big 'beefsteak' or Marmande tomatoes weigh 175-200 g/6-7 oz each. Try imported Plum tomatoes too. Home grown available April to October.

Celery – look for firm, unblemished sticks. Use the leaves as a garnish. Available all year round.

Cucumber – choose from the more familiar smooth-skinned cucumber, or the short, fat, spiny-skinned ridge cucumber, popular on the Continent. Ridge cucumbers are coarser in texture and should be peeled before use. Available all year round, home grown March to October.

Beetroot – buy raw and boil for around 25 minutes according to size, until tender. Add to salads at the last minute to prevent colour transferring to other ingredients. Available all year round.

Potatoes – waxy varieties are best for salads. Ask your greengrocer's advice. Available all year round, new from June to September.

White and red cabbage – tight heads of firm crisp cabbage. They keep in the fridge for two or three weeks. They need to be finely shredded when eaten raw as they can be indigestible. Available all year round.

Mushrooms – cultivated types include tiny, tightly closed button mushrooms, larger and more open caps and flat field mushrooms. The larger blacker mushrooms have more flavour, but tend to discolour salads. Just wipe mushrooms before slicing and serving. Available all year round.

Radish – Summer varieties have a crisp texture and peppery flavour. They are popular as a garnish. Available all year round.

Spring onions – strongly flavoured green onions, used mainly as a garnish. Available all year round.

Shallots – although a member of the onion family, they grow rather like garlic in clusters of cloves. They are usually pale purple in colour and mild in taste. Available September to January.

Onions – British main crop onions are generally rather fierce – they make your eyes water for a start! Big, mild Spanish onions are a better choice for eating raw. Red Italian onions are quite mild and look pretty in salads. Available all year round.

... AND THE MORE EXOTIC

*Spaghetti squash – looks rather like
an elongated pumpkin or yellow
marrow. When cooked, the flesh can
be removed in spaghetti-like strands –
hence the name.
Imported, available
August to December.*

*Artichokes, Globe – choose young
tender ones and poach before eating.
(see page 22).
Available all year round, cheapest
June to September.*

*Mange-tout – also known as snow
peas. They look like flat peapods and
have a crisp texture and a sweet,
fresh taste.
Imported, available May to August.*

*Okra – looks like rough-skinned
ribbed chillies, tapering to a point.
To use, cut off the caps without
exposing the seeds. When cooked,
they exude a slightly slimy substance,
but this disappears after 10 minutes
or so of cooking.
Imported, available June to
September.*

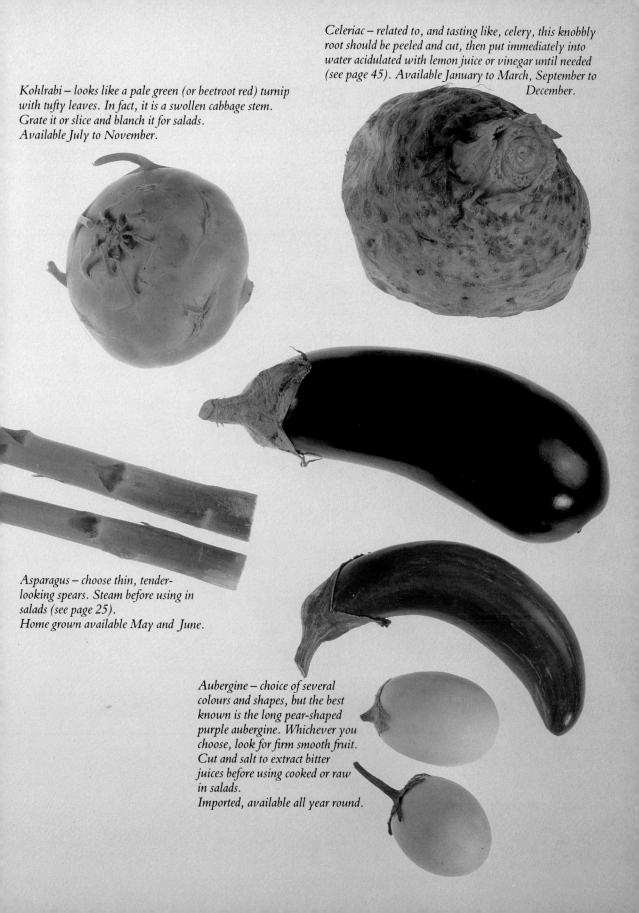

Kohlrabi – looks like a pale green (or beetroot red) turnip with tufty leaves. In fact, it is a swollen cabbage stem. Grate it or slice and blanch it for salads. Available July to November.

Celeriac – related to, and tasting like, celery, this knobbly root should be peeled and cut, then put immediately into water acidulated with lemon juice or vinegar until needed (see page 45). Available January to March, September to December.

Asparagus – choose thin, tender-looking spears. Steam before using in salads (see page 25). Home grown available May and June.

Aubergine – choice of several colours and shapes, but the best known is the long pear-shaped purple aubergine. Whichever you choose, look for firm smooth fruit. Cut and salt to extract bitter juices before using cooked or raw in salads. Imported, available all year round.

Peppers – the green ones have a slightly bitter and distinctive flavour, while the red ones are sweeter, the pretty yellow ones sweeter still. Cut off the tops and discard the seeds before slicing into rings. Hot Bonnet peppers are smaller, more fluted and hot-tasting. Chillies come from the same capsicum family. As a general rule, the smaller the pepper, the hotter it is. The seeds are the hottest part, so they are usually discarded. Take care not to touch your eyes or mouth after handling chillies as they have an irritant effect. Available all year round.

Japanese radish – also called mooli or daikon. Looks like a long, white, whiskery root and tastes slightly peppery. Imported, available all year round.

Avocado – two varieties are available. Hass avocados have black knobbly skins and are rather short and stubby. Fuerte avocados are green and pear-shaped. Imported, available all year round.

Fresh herbs – enliven salads. Add basil to tomato salads, chives, parsley or mint to potato, savory to bean salads, coriander, parsley or tarragon to green salads.

Green cauliflower – a pretty green version of a favourite vegetable. Purple cauliflowers are sometimes available too. Home grown, available July to September.

Sweet corn – look out for baby corn cobs to use whole or sliced in salads. Imported, available July to September.

Fennel – looks like a short, plump head of celery with fine green leaves. Tastes like aniseed. Use the leaves to garnish salads. Imported, available all year round.

Courgettes – baby marrows with tender edible skin and a sweet, fresh flavour. Look out for yellow-skinned varieties too. Available all year, home grown July to August.

Nasturtiums – the brilliant orange flowers, picked from your garden (or sometimes found in supermarkets) are edible. They look pretty in salads, but taste hot and peppery. Available July and August.

SPROUTING YOUR OWN BEANS, GRAINS AND SEEDS

The bean sprouts that are most familiar to us are grown from mung beans. Like a lot of other beans, seeds and grains, they are easy to grow at home and make delicious salads (see pages 48-49). All you need is one large wide-necked jar, a piece of cheesecloth, and an elastic band.

What to do
Wash the beans; pick over and discard damaged ones and any stones. Put enough into the jar to fill it one-quarter full. Fill the jar with cold water and cover with the cheesecloth, securing it with the elastic band. Leave overnight. The next day, drain the beans and discard any that have not absorbed water. Return to the jar, lay it on its side and cover with a tea towel (light can make the sprouts taste bitter). Allow 2 to 3 days for sprouts to grow, but rinse the sprouts twice every day, draining them thoroughly each time and returning them to the jar. Use when the sprouts are about 4 cm/1½ inches long.

What to sprout

Aduki Beans: Small red beans, easy to sprout, they take about five days. Mild, slightly sweet flavour, similar to mung beans.

Alfalfa Seeds: Tiny seeds which take about three days to grow into fine cress-like sprouts.

Black-eyed Beans: Allow about four days for these crisp and slightly bitter tasting bean sprouts to grow.

Chickpeas: These swell during soaking, then take about five days to produce sweetish-tasting sprouts. Eat when about 6 cm/2½ inches long.

Fenugreek: Spicy seeds that take three or four days to sprout. Eat them while they are still short for maximum spiciness.

Flageolet: Pale green kidney-shaped beans, they take about four days to sprout and are fresh-tasting, like garden peas.

Haricot Beans: You'll have firm, crisp and delicious sprouts after three or four days.

Lentils: You'll need whole green lentils; split ones won't sprout. They take four to six days and have a nutty flavour.

Mung Beans: The most familiar Chinese bean sprout. They take about five days to grow to about 10 cm/ 4 inches long.

Soya Beans: These will take up to three days to grow to the desired 2.5-cm/1-inch length. They are prone to fermentation, so rinse them more frequently and sprout in the refrigerator, covered to keep out the light.

Sunflower Seeds: Choose hulled seeds and allow two to three days. Eat while short, or they can taste bitter.

Wheat: Use whole grain wheat and harvest it after two or three days when the sprout is only as long as the grain. After this time the appearance and texture deteriorate.

SALAD DRESSINGS

All salads need a dressing to moisten and lubricate them, bind disparate ingredients together, and to add extra flavour. Match the dressing carefully to the salad and use good quality ingredients to get the best results. Whether you're making the simple but classic Vinaigrette or your own mayonnaise, (see page 18) the type and quality of vinegar and oil that you choose will influence the taste of the finished dressing and make or mar it.

For both types of dressing the way to success is to be a miser with the vinegar — use it very sparingly — and a spendthrift with the oil — use it generously. Use a ratio of about five parts oil to one part vinegar — but taste the dressing and adjust these proportions accordingly.

Which oil to choose?
Olive Oil: Available in different qualities. Extra virgin oil comes from the first cold pressing of the olives. It's a yellowish green heavy oil with a distinctive taste. Virgin olive oil is paler in colour and not so heavy or strong tasting. Keep tightly sealed in a cool, dark place for up to one year.
Sunflower, Corn, Safflower or Soya Oil: Lighter multi-purpose oils that are rather bland tasting. Sunflower and safflower are high in polyunsaturated fats.
Walnut, Hazelnut or Almond Oil: These nut-based oils are light, aromatic and distinctly nutty in flavour – excellent on green salads. They are expensive and must be refrigerated if they are to retain their fresh flavour.

. . . and which vinegar?
Acid in the form of vinegar or lemon adds a note of sharpness to a dressing which heightens the flavour.
Wine Vinegar: Red or white wine vinegars are light and fresh and complement most dressings without overpowering them.
Cider Vinegar: This vinegar produced from apples is suitable for most types of salad.
Herb Vinegars: Make your own by infusing a sprig of fresh herbs, such as tarragon or rosemary, in white wine or cider vinegar. Use selectively in complementary salads rather than as general purpose vinegar.

Malt Vinegar: This vinegar is not suitable for salads as it has a high acetic acid content and a harsh taste.
Fruit Vinegars: Raspberry is probably the best known. They are made by steeping fruit in vinegar, then adding sugar to the strained liquid. Use them in delicate green salads.

VINAIGRETTE DRESSING
Makes 150 ml/¼ pint

2 tablespoons vinegar
¼ teaspoon salt
freshly ground black pepper
pinch of mustard powder
8 tablespoons oil

Put all the ingredients into a bowl and mix together, or put them in a screw-top jar and shake well until emulsified. Taste and adjust seasoning if necessary. Store in a jar in the refrigerator. Shake well before using.

Vinaigrette Variations
Garlic: Add 1 peeled and crushed garlic clove to the dressing.
Herb: Add 1 to 2 tablespoons chopped parsley, tarragon, basil or other fresh herb of your choice. If using dried herbs, add only 1 teaspoon, and allow to steep in the dressing before using.
Lemon: Use 2 tablespoons lemon juice in place of the vinegar. Add the grated rind too, if you require a stronger flavour. Make orange or lime dressing in the same way.
Mustard: Add 2 to 3 teaspoons coarse-grained mustard to the dressing.
Watercress: Add a handful of trimmed and chopped watercress to the dressing.
Sesame seed: Grill 1 to 2 tablespoons sesame seeds until pale golden. Add to the dressing.
Walnut: Add 25 g/1 oz finely chopped walnuts to the dressing.

MAYONNAISE...

BASIC MAYONNAISE
Makes 150 ml/¼ pint

2 egg yolks, at room temperature
1-2 teaspoons vinegar
pinch of mustard powder
150 ml/¼ pint oil
salt and freshly ground black pepper

Put the egg yolks, mustard, and 1 teaspoon of the vinegar in a bowl. Mix well with a hand whisk, and start adding the oil a few drops at a time. Beat constantly while adding the oil in a fine trickle, until the mixture is thick and creamy. Taste and add more vinegar if required. Add salt and pepper.

Liquidiser Method
Blend the oil, mustard and vinegar for 10 seconds. Remove the central cap from the liquidiser lid and add the oil, drop by drop, as the machine is running. Taste and adjust seasoning.

If the mayonnaise curdles
Curdling can occur if the eggs are too cold, or if you add the oil too quickly. Whisk in one tablespoon boiling water. If this fails, put another egg yolk into a clean bowl and beat in the curdled mixture drop by drop. Add an extra three to four tablespoons oil too, to give the right consistency.

Mayonnaise variations
Garlic: Add 1 peeled and crushed garlic clove to the completed mayonnaise.
Herb: Add 2 to 3 tablespoons chopped fresh dill, parsley or other herb of your choice to the completed mayonnaise.
Green: Add chopped watercress or spring onions to the mayonnaise.
Tomato: Add 1 tablespoon tomato purée and a squeeze of lemon juice to completed mayonnaise.
Lemon: Use lemon juice instead of vinegar to make mayonnaise. Add grated rind too, if a stronger flavour is required.
Thousand Island: Add 1 chopped hard-boiled egg, 1 teaspoon each of chopped red pepper, spring onions and parsley and 3-4 drops of Tabasco to 150 ml/¼ pint mayonnaise. Serve with crisp lettuce salads.

...AND OTHER DRESSINGS

Yogurt

Choose a 'set' or Greek yogurt. Add a squeeze of lemon juice and seasoning to taste. Use half and half with mayonnaise to make a lighter dressing for coleslaw or potato salad.

Sour Cream

Add a squeeze of lemon juice and 1 tablespoon chopped chives to 150 ml/¼ pint soured cream. Season to taste. Excellent on potato or beetroot salads.

Blue Cheese

Mash, or liquidise 50 g/2 oz Danish Blue or Stilton cheese with 150 ml/¼ pint single cream. Add a squeeze of lemon juice and season to taste. Good with green, apple or celery salads.

SALADS FOR STARTERS

RATATOUILLE
Serves 6

1 large aubergine, cut into cubes
salt
6 tablespoons olive oil
1 large onion, chopped
2 large courgettes, sliced
1 large green pepper, seeded and sliced
397-g/14-oz can tomatoes
2 cloves garlic, crushed
freshly ground black pepper

Put the aubergine into a colander, sprinkle with salt and leave for 30 minutes to extract the bitter juices. Rinse, drain and squeeze out thoroughly. Heat the oil in a saucepan and add the onions. Fry until transparent. Add the aubergine and cook for a further 10 minutes. Add the remaining ingredients and seasoning. Cover and simmer for about 20 minutes, stirring from time to time. Adjust seasoning. Serve hot or cold with plenty of crusty bread to mop up the juices.

MEXICAN AVOCADO
Serves 6

2 large ripe avocados, peeled and cut into cubes
3 tablespoons oil
1 tablespoon lemon juice
1 clove garlic, crushed
3 or 4 drops Tabasco
3 medium-sized tomatoes, peeled
½ yellow pepper, cut into strips
1 slice Spanish onion, chopped
salt and freshly ground black pepper
tortilla chips

Put the cubed avocados immediately into a bowl with the oil, lemon juice, garlic and Tabasco. Toss lightly. Cut the tomatoes into thin wedges, discarding the seeds. Add with the yellow pepper and onion to the avocado. Toss together gently until coated with dressing. Taste and season, adding more Tabasco if liked. Divide between individual plates and serve with tortilla chips.

SPICED CUCUMBER SALAD
Serves 6

2 cucumbers
1 tablespoon salt
1 clove garlic, crushed
2 small, fresh red chillies, thinly sliced
4 tablespoons oil
3 tablespoons white wine vinegar
2 tablespoons sugar
3 tablespoons soy sauce

Cut the cucumbers in half lengthways. Peel off the skin and scrape out the seeds with a teaspoon. Cut each half into 2.5-cm/1-inch lengths, put into a colander and sprinkle with salt. Leave for 1 hour. Squeeze cucumber to remove excess liquid. Put into a heatproof serving dish with the garlic and most of the sliced chillies. Heat the oil and vinegar until almost boiling, add the sugar and stir until dissolved. Pour over the cucumber. Allow to stand for 3 hours. Add reserved chillies to soy sauce and serve with the salad as a dip.

TOMATOES WITH MOZZARELLA
Serves 6

3 firm beefsteak tomatoes, sliced
225 g/8 oz mozzarella cheese, thinly sliced
1 small onion, thinly sliced
5 tablespoons olive oil
50 g/2 oz small black olives
freshly ground black pepper

Arrange the sliced tomatoes and mozzarella alternately on a shallow serving dish. Separate the onion slices into rings, scatter over the top with the black olives. Trickle the oil over the whole salad and grind a little black pepper over. Leave for about 1 hour before serving with hot crusty bread.

ARTICHOKES WITH PRAWNS AND HOLLANDAISE
Serves 6

3 globe artichokes
½ lemon
350 g/12 oz whole prawns
1 onion, sliced

Hollandaise Sauce
1 tablespoon lemon juice
3 egg yolks
225 g/8 oz butter, melted and cooled
salt and freshly ground pepper

Cut away stalks from the artichokes and snip off tips of leaves. Cook in boiling, lightly salted water with the lemon and onion for 30 minutes. Drain upside down on a plate and leave to cool completely. Prepare the prawns by removing heads and body shells, but leaving the tails on. Pull the leaves off the artichokes and reserve. Cut away and discard the hairy 'chokes' from the centres. Cut the artichoke bottoms into slices. Arrange artichoke leaves and bottoms on individual plates with the prawns, leaving a space for the sauce.

To make the hollandaise, beat the lemon juice, egg yolks and seasoning in a bowl over a pan of barely simmering water. Gradually beat in the butter a trickle at a time. Continue until all the butter is added and the sauce has the consistency of thick double cream. Adjust the seasoning to taste. Divide the sauce between the plates and serve immediately.

SPAGHETTI SQUASH SALAD
Serves 6

This new vegetable from the squash family comes from Israel and looks like a fat yellow marrow. After cooking, the flesh looks just like 'spaghetti', but it will keep your dinner guests guessing.

1 spaghetti squash
300 ml/½ pint soured cream
1 tablespoon snipped chives
50-g/2-oz jar black lumpfish roe
50-g/2-oz jar red lumpfish roe
salt and freshly ground black pepper

Cut the fruit in half around the centre. Scoop out the seeds with a spoon and discard. Cook both halves in a large pan of boiling, lightly salted water for 20 minutes. Drain thoroughly and scrape out the strings of flesh with a fork. Put into a large bowl and allow to cool. Add the soured cream, chives and most of the lumpfish roe, reserving a little to garnish. Toss together lightly and season to taste. Divide between individual plates and garnish with the reserved lumpfish roe.

MARINATED MUSHROOMS
Serves 6

5 tablespoons olive oil
1 large onion, chopped
675 g/1½ lb small button mushrooms
2 cloves garlic, crushed
150 ml/¼ pint red wine
1 tablespoon tomato purée
½ teaspoon sugar
salt and freshly ground black pepper
flat-leafed parsley

Heat the oil in a large saucepan. Add the onions and fry until transparent. Increase the heat and add the mushrooms. Fry for 5 minutes, turning frequently. Reduce the heat; add the garlic, wine, tomato purée, sugar and plenty of seasoning. Cover and simmer for 10 minutes. Allow to cool completely before serving. Season to taste and divide between individual plates. Sprinkle with snipped flat-leafed parsley. Serve with crusty bread to mop up the juices.

AVOCADO WITH PINE NUTS
Serves 6

50 g/2 oz pine nuts
3 avocados, peeled, halved and stones
  removed
3 tablespoons lemon juice
sprigs of curly endive, to garnish
1 quantity of Vinaigrette Dressing
  (see page 16)

Put the pine nuts into a non-stick pan and cook over a moderate heat for 3-5 minutes, shaking the pan occasionally, until the pine nuts are pale golden. Place each avocado half cut-side down on an individual plate. Cut lengthways into thin slices, but leave the slices joined at the top end. Pull the slices apart slightly so that they make avocado 'fans'. Brush with lemon juice. Garnish each plate with a sprig of curly endive. Spoon the dressing over the avocados, sprinkle the pine nuts on top and serve immediately.

MELON WITH SMOKED SALMON
Serves 6

2 small ripe Ogen melons
150 ml/¼ pint double cream
1 sprig fresh dill, snipped
175 g/6 oz sliced smoked salmon
salt and freshly ground black pepper

Halve the melons and discard the seeds. Cut the flesh away from the skin, then cut it into cubes. Put the melon into a salad bowl with the cream and the dill. Cut the salmon into fine strips. Reserve half of it to garnish. Stir the rest into the salad and season to taste. Divide the salad between individual plates and scatter the reserved salmon over it. Serve with sliced brown bread and butter.

BASQUE SALAD
Serves 6

1 small stale French stick
2 beefsteak tomatoes
1 mild Spanish onion, thinly sliced
1 quantity of Vinaigrette Dressing
  (see page 16)
50-g/2 oz-can anchovy fillets
6 tablespoons milk
75 g/3 oz stuffed green olives
flat-leafed parsley

Cut the bread into 1-cm/½-inch slices and arrange in a single layer on a large serving platter. Slice the tomatoes and cut each slice into quarters. Arrange on top of the bread with the onion. Pour the dressing over and leave to soak for 1 hour. Drain the anchovies and soak in the milk for 30 minutes to remove some of the saltiness. Drain and snip into pieces over the salad. Scatter the olives and parsley over the salad and serve.

LOLLO ROSSO LETTUCE, GRAPES AND STILTON
Serves 6

1 Lollo Rosso lettuce
1 quantity of Vinaigrette Dressing
  (see page 16)
350 g/12 oz black grapes, halved and seeded
175 g/6 oz Stilton cheese
50 g/2 oz pecans or walnuts, roughly chopped

Separate the lettuce leaves and tear them into manageable pieces. Put half the dressing into a bowl. Add the lettuce and toss well. Divide between individual plates. Put the remaining dressing into the bowl and add the grapes. Cut the Stilton into neat cubes, discarding the rind. Add to the bowl with the nuts. Toss well. Arrange on the plates with the lettuce and serve immediately.

ASPARAGUS AND MANGE-TOUT WITH HORSERADISH
Serves 6

24 asparagus spears
225 g/8 oz mange-tout, topped and tailed
150 ml/¼ pint double cream
2 tablespoons creamed horseradish
salt and freshly ground black pepper

Trim off the woody ends of the asparagus. Place the spears in a colander over a pan of boiling water. Cover and steam for 5-7 minutes, until tender. Drain on absorbent kitchen paper. Steam the mange-tout in the same way for 3 minutes. Leave to cool. Whip the cream until it forms soft peaks, fold in the horseradish and season to taste. Arrange some of each vegetable on individual plates and spoon the dressing next to it. Eat with your fingers, dipping the asparagus and mange-tout into the dressing.

SALAD OF WARM CHICKEN LIVERS
Serves 6

225 g/8 oz chicken livers
1 head radicchio
1 yellow pepper, seeded
½ cucumber, peeled
2 tablespoons oil
salt and freshly ground black pepper
6 tablespoons dry white vermouth

Separate chicken livers and trim, discarding any membranes. Separate the radicchio into leaves and tear into manageable pieces. Cut yellow pepper into strips. Cut cucumber in half lengthways; scoop out the seeds with a teaspoon. Slice thinly. Put vegetables into a bowl with the seasoning and half the oil. Toss until lightly coated. Divide between individual plates. Just before serving, heat the rest of the oil in a frying pan. Add the livers and fry over a high heat for 2 minutes until browned, but still moist and juicy. Add the vermouth and bring to the boil, stirring to dissolve any sediment. Season generously and spoon over the salad. Serve immediately with French bread.

COURGETTE, PINK GRAPEFRUIT AND PARMA HAM
Serves 6

450 g/1 lb yellow or green courgettes, sliced
4 tablespoons oil
salt and freshly ground black pepper
2 pink grapefruit
100 g/4 oz Parma ham

Steam the courgette slices in a colander over boiling water for 4 minutes, turning once or twice during cooking. Put the oil and plenty of seasoning into a heatproof bowl. Stir in the hot courgettes and leave to cool and absorb the dressing. Cut a slice from the top and bottom of the grapefruit. Using a serrated knife, cut away the rind and white pith in strips. Hold the grapefruit over a plate to catch the juice and cut between the membranes to remove whole segments. Discard any pips. Stir grapefruit lightly into the courgettes. Season to taste. Divide between individual plates. Cut the ham into strips and scatter over the salads.

SIMPLE CAESAR SALAD

Serves 6

2 cloves garlic, crushed
150 ml/¼ pint oil
3 thick slices wholemeal bread
4 Little Gem lettuce hearts
2 teaspoons lemon juice
2 tablespoons olive oil
¼ teaspoon Tabasco sauce
25 g/1 oz grated Parmesan cheese
salt and freshly ground black pepper
2 eggs, at room temperature

Crush the garlic into the oil and leave for 1 hour so that the oil takes on the flavour. Remove the crusts from the bread and cut into neat cubes. Strain the oil into a frying pan, add the bread cubes a few at a time and fry until crisp and golden. Remove with a slotted spoon and drain on absorbent kitchen paper. Separate the lettuce leaves and tear them into manageable pieces. Mix the lemon juice, olive oil, Tabasco sauce, Parmesan cheese and seasoning in the salad bowl. Put in the crossed salad servers and pile the lettuce leaves on top of them. Add the eggs to boiling water and boil for 2 minutes. Toss the salad in the dressing, break the eggs over the salad and toss the salad lightly. Scatter the garlic croutons over the salad and serve immediately.

SPINACH WITH BACON AND AVOCADO

Serves 6

6 rashers rindless streaky bacon
¼ red pepper
¾ quantity of Vinaigrette Dressing (see page 16)
2 small ripe avocados, halved, pitted and peeled
350 g/12 oz small, tender spinach leaves
salt and freshly ground black pepper

Grill the bacon until crisp; cut into strips with kitchen scissors. Cut fine strips of red pepper, using a canelle knife. Leave them in cold water for 10 minutes until curled. Make the Vinaigrette Dressing in a large bowl. Cut the avocado into thick slices; put into the dressing with the spinach leaves and seasoning. Turn gently until coated with dressing. Divide between individual plates and sprinkle the bacon and drained red pepper curls over the salads just before serving.

SIDE SALADS

GREEN SALAD
Serves 4 to 6

Order a green salad in France, and you'll get a simple dish of dressed lettuce. There is nothing at all wrong with that provided that the lettuce is dry and crisp and the dressing is perfect!

¾ quantity of Vinaigrette Dressing
(see page 16)
1 lettuce (see pages 4–5)
1 tablespoon chopped parsley
1 tablespoon chopped tarragon
1 tablespoon chopped chives

Wash the lettuce, separating it into leaves. Dry thoroughly, patting in absorbent kitchen paper or using a salad spinner. Tear lettuce into manageable pieces; do not cut it or the edges will turn brown. Put the Vinaigrette Dressing in a large salad bowl. Put the salad servers into the bowl, crossing them over. Put the lettuce on top of the servers and sprinkle the herbs over. Toss in the dressing just before serving.

MIXED LEAVES
Serves 6

½ Webb's lettuce
½ oak leaf lettuce
½ Quattro Stagione lettuce
100 g/4 oz spinach
few dandelion leaves (optional)
few nasturtium flowers (optional)
1 quantity of Vinaigrette Dressing
(see page 16)

Carefully wash all leaves and dry thoroughly. Make the Vinaigrette Dressing in a large salad bowl. Put in the crossed salad servers and pile the leaves on top of them. Toss the leaves in the dressing just before serving. Garnish with nasturtium flowers if liked.

CHINESE LEAVES WITH PEANUT DRESSING
Serves 6

225 g/8 oz Chinese leaves, trimmed
100 g/4 oz bean sprouts
3 tablespoons crunchy peanut butter
1 tablespoon soy sauce
½ teaspoon anchovy essence (optional)
pinch of chilli powder
1 teaspoon sugar
150 ml/¼ pint boiling water

Cut Chinese leaves into 2.5-cm/1-inch slices. Put into a salad bowl with the bean sprouts. Put the peanut butter into a small pan with the soy sauce, anchovy essence, chilli powder, sugar and water. Heat gently, stirring until evenly mixed. Pour over the salad, toss well and serve while still warm.

BITTER GREENS
Serves 6

1 quantity of Vinaigrette Dressing
  (see page 16)
1 head curly endive
1 small radicchio
1 head chicory, thinly sliced

Make the dressing in a large bowl. Put in the crossed salad servers. Tear the curly endive and radicchio into manageable pieces. Wash and dry thoroughly. Pile on top of the salad servers with the sliced chicory. Toss leaves in dressing just before serving.

TOMATO, ONION AND BASIL
Serves 6

4 large beefsteak tomatoes, sliced
½ mild Spanish onion, thinly sliced
8 fresh basil leaves, chopped or ½ teaspoon dried basil
1 quantity of Vinaigrette Dressing (see page 16)
salt and freshly ground black pepper

Arrange the tomatoes and onions on a shallow dish. If using dried basil, stir it into the Vinaigrette Dressing, then spoon the dressing over the salad. Leave for about 1 hour. If using fresh basil, snip it into strips over the dressed salad just before serving. Season to taste.

ITALIAN TOMATO AND FENNEL
Serves 6

2 beefsteak tomatoes, sliced
1 red onion, thinly sliced
1 fennel bulb, trimmed and thinly sliced
4 tablespoons olive oil
1 tablespoon lemon juice
salt and freshly ground black pepper

Arrange the sliced tomatoes, onions and fennel on a shallow serving dish. Mix the olive oil with the lemon juice and seasonings, and trickle it over the mixed vegetables. Leave for 1 hour before serving.

TOMATO AND COURGETTE
Serves 6

5 tablespoons oil
225 g/8 oz courgettes, thinly sliced
1 clove garlic, crushed
6 medium-sized tomatoes, peeled
2 teaspoons white wine vinegar
salt and freshly ground black pepper
3 tablespoons chopped parsley

Heat the oil in a frying pan. Add the courgettes and fry gently until tender but not browned. Add the crushed garlic and cook for 1 minute. Cut the tomatoes into wedges, discarding seeds. Put into a heatproof salad bowl and pour the contents of the frying pan over the tomatoes. Add the vinegar and seasoning and toss gently. Sprinkle with the chopped parsley and serve while the salad is still warm.

OKRA AND TOMATO
Serves 6

Make sure that you choose young tender okra. It can be fibrous and tough when older. Trim off the stalk end, but take care not to expose the seeds.

3 tablespoons oil
1 large onion, chopped
1 clove garlic, crushed
350 g/12 oz okra, trimmed
397-g/14-oz can of tomatoes
1 teaspoon sugar
salt and freshly ground black pepper
flat-leafed parsley, chopped

Heat the oil in a frying pan or flameproof casserole. Add the onion and garlic and fry until transparent. Add the okra and cook for about 5 minutes until it changes colour. Add the canned tomatoes and juice, the sugar, salt and pepper. Cover and cook gently for about 15 minutes until the okra is tender. Allow to cool and serve sprinkled with the chopped parsley.

COLESLAW
Serves 6 to 8

450 g/1 lb white cabbage, finely shredded
1 small onion, thinly sliced
2 sticks celery, thinly sliced
3 large carrots, peeled and grated
1 quantity of Basic Mayonnaise (see page 18)
salt and freshly ground black pepper

Put the shredded cabbage into a large bowl with the onion, celery and grated carrot. Mix together. Pour on the mayonnaise, season and toss thoroughly until salad is evenly coated. Leave for 1 hour to soften slightly before serving.

CARROT, COURGETTE AND SESAME
Serves 6

350 g/12 oz carrots, cut into matchsticks
225 g/8 oz courgettes, cut into matchsticks
1 tablespoon oil
3 tablespoons orange juice
salt and freshly ground black pepper
2 tablespoons sesame seeds

Steam the carrots in a covered colander over a pan of boiling water for 2 minutes. Add the courgette matchsticks and steam for a further 2 minutes. Tip into a salad bowl, add the oil and orange juice, season and toss well. Put the sesame seeds into a non-stick frying pan and dry fry over a gentle heat until golden. Sprinkle over the salad just before serving.

RED SLAW
Serves 6

3 large oranges
450 g/1 lb red cabbage, finely shredded
1 teaspoon caraway seeds
⅓ quantity of Basic Mayonnaise (see page 18)
3 tablespoons natural yogurt
salt and freshly ground black pepper

Cut a slice from the top and bottom of each orange. Using a serrated knife, cut away peel and white pith in strips. Hold the oranges over a large bowl to catch the juice, and cut between the membranes to remove whole segments. Discard any pips. Add the shredded cabbage to the orange segments with the caraway seeds, mayonnaise and yogurt. Toss together lightly until evenly coated. Season to taste.

SUNSET BEETROOT
Serves 6

4 small oranges
1 quantity of Vinaigrette Dressing (see page 16)
450 g/1 lb cooked beetroot, sliced

Grate the rind from one of the oranges into the vinaigrette dressing and reserve. Cut a slice from the top and bottom of the oranges. Using a serrated knife, cut away peel and white pith in strips. Cut the oranges into slices, discarding any pips. Arrange the beetroot and orange slices on a serving dish. Spoon the dressing over just before serving.

TRADITIONAL POTATO SALAD
Serves 6

650 g/1½ lb potatoes
salt
1 quantity of Basic Mayonnaise (see page 18)
1 tablespoon chopped chives
freshly ground black pepper

Boil the whole unpeeled potatoes in lightly salted water for 15-20 minutes until tender. Allow to cool, then peel. Cut into neat cubes and put into a bowl. Add the mayonnaise, chives and seasoning. Toss gently until evenly coated.

HOT POTATOES WITH BACON
Serves 6

900 g/2 lb small new potatoes
salt and freshly ground black pepper
4 rashers rindless streaky bacon
2 tablespoons sesame seeds
1 quantity of Vinaigrette Dressing
(see page 16)
2 tablespoons chopped parsley

Scrub the potatoes and cook in lightly salted boiling water for about 15 minutes until tender. Meanwhile, grill the bacon until crisp. Remove and snip into pieces. Spread sesame seeds on a piece of kitchen foil and grill until pale golden. Make vinaigrette in a salad bowl. Drain potatoes thoroughly and add to the dressing with sesame seeds, parsley and seasoning. Toss together gently. Scatter bacon over the salad and serve while still warm.

POTATOES WITH FRENCH BEANS
Serves 6

650 g/1½ lb small new potatoes
salt
225 g/8 oz French beans, topped and tailed
1 quantity of Vinaigrette Dressing
(see page 16)
1 teaspoon coarse-grained mustard
1 shallot, finely chopped
12 small black olives
1 tablespoon chopped parsley
freshly ground black pepper

Scrub the potatoes, put into lightly salted boiling water. Bring to the boil again and cook until tender. Meanwhile, cut each bean into 3 or 4 pieces. Put them into a colander and steam over the potatoes for 5 minutes. Put the vinaigrette, mustard, shallots, olives and parsley into a salad bowl. Drain the potatoes, add, with the beans, to the dressing. Season. Toss until coated and serve while still warm.

HOT SPICED POTATOES
Serves 6

900 g/2 lb potatoes, peeled
salt
5 tablespoons oil
2 tablespoons sesame seeds
2.5-cm/1-inch piece root ginger, peeled and
**   chopped**
2 fresh green chillies, thinly sliced
2 tablespoons lemon juice
1 tablespoon chopped fresh green coriander

Cut potatoes into thick slices. Cook in boiling, lightly salted water until just tender. Drain well and put into a heatproof salad bowl. Heat the oil in a frying pan, add the seeds, ginger, and sliced chillies. Cook for 2-3 minutes, stirring occasionally. Add the lemon juice and pour the dressing over the salad. Toss together and allow to cool. Stir in the coriander leaves just before serving.

POTATOES WITH PARMA HAM
Serves 6

650 g/1½ lb small new potatoes
salt
100 g/4 oz Parma ham
150 ml/¼ pint double cream
grated rind of 1 lemon
2 teaspoons lemon juice
1 teaspoon chopped fresh dill
freshly ground black pepper

Scrub the potatoes and cook in boiling, lightly salted water for 10-15 minutes until tender. Drain and leave until cool enough to handle. Cut into slices and divide between individual plates. Cut the ham into strips and scatter over the potatoes. Mix the cream, lemon rind, lemon juice, dill and black pepper together. Spoon a little of the dressing over each salad and serve immediately.

MUSHROOMS WITH SOY DRESSING
Serves 6

Marinating the mushrooms in the dressing for an hour before serving makes them plump and moist.

450 g/1 lb large button mushrooms, thickly sliced
6 tablespoons oil
2 tablespoons soy sauce
black peppercorns, roughly crushed

Put the sliced mushrooms into a large bowl. Add oil and soy sauce, toss well and leave for 1 hour, turning the mushrooms occasionally. The mushrooms, themselves, will make a lot of juice. Add black pepper to taste. You may not need to add salt because of the soy sauce. Serve with bread.

ORANGE AND WATERCRESS
Serves 6

3 medium-sized oranges
1 bunch watercress
3 tablespoons olive oil
2 teaspoons lemon juice
freshly ground black pepper

Cut a slice from the top and bottom of the oranges. Using a serrated knife cut away peel and white pith in strips. Cut between the membranes to remove whole segments, discarding any pips. Tear the watercress into manageable pieces, and arrange it with the oranges on a serving dish. Mix oil and lemon juice, spoon over the salad and add a little freshly ground black pepper.

CUCUMBER AND YOGURT

Serves 4 to 6

**1 large cucumber, halved lengthways and
  sliced**
salt
150 ml/¼ pint natural yogurt
**2 sprigs fresh mint, finely chopped or 1
  teaspoon concentrated bottled mint**
½ teaspoon paprika

Layer the cucumber slices in a colander, sprinkling
each layer with a little salt. Let drain for 1 hour. Press
lightly to squeeze out excess fluid and put into a
bowl. Add the yogurt and mint and stir together
lightly. Serve with a sprinkling of paprika.

WALDORF SALAD

Serves 6

4 Cox's apples, quartered, cored and sliced
2 tablespoons lemon juice
6 sticks celery, trimmed and sliced
50 g/2 oz walnuts, chopped
1 quantity of Basic Mayonnaise (see page 18)
salt and freshly ground black pepper

Put the apple slices immediately into a bowl with the
lemon juice, to prevent discolouration. Add the
celery, walnuts and mayonnaise. Toss gently and
season to taste. Line a salad bowl with lettuce leaves,
and arrange the salad in the centre.

GREEN RICE
Serves 6

350 g/12 oz long grain rice
salt
100 g/4 oz frozen petits pois
6 spring onions, thinly sliced
½ bunch watercress
5 tablespoons oil
2 tablespoons lemon juice
freshly ground black pepper

Rinse the rice with cold water; then cook in boiling, lightly salted water for 12-15 minutes until just tender. Steam the peas in a colander over the rice for 3 minutes. Drain the rice and peas, rinse with cold water and drain thoroughly. Put into a large bowl with the spring onion. Discard the coarse stalks from the watercress. Put the watercress into a liquidiser with the oil and lemon juice and blend until finely chopped. Pour over the salad and toss lightly together. Season to taste.

TOMATO RICE
Serves 6

350 g/12 oz long grain rice
397-g/ 14-oz can tomatoes, chopped
salt
5 tablespoons oil
1 large onion, finely chopped
1 clove garlic, crushed
100 g/4 oz small button mushrooms, quartered
1 tablespoon red wine vinegar
1 tablespoon chopped parsley
freshly ground black pepper

Rinse the rice with cold water and put into a saucepan. Add the canned tomatoes and juice, one can of water and a little salt. Bring to the boil and simmer for 12-15 minutes until the rice is tender and has absorbed the liquid. Meanwhile, heat the oil in a frying pan and fry the onion gently until transparent. Add the garlic and mushrooms and fry for 3 minutes. Add vinegar and parsley to the pan; then pour the contents over the rice. Toss together lightly and season to taste.

TAMARIND RICE
Serves 6

Tamarind is a date-like fruit much used in Indian cooking. You will find the dried unsweetened pulp in Indian shops. Soak it, and use the slighly acidic liquid that results in this salad and also in curries.

50 g/2 oz tamarind pulp
350 g/12 oz basmati rice
salt
4 tablespoons oil
2 teaspoons yellow mustard seeds
1 teaspoon cumin seeds
2 teaspoons coriander seeds
50 g/2 oz flaked almonds
2 fresh chillies, thinly sliced
few fresh coriander leaves, chopped
freshly ground black pepper

Put the tamarind in a small bowl and cover with cold water. Leave to soak for 1 hour, stirring occasionally. Strain through a fine sieve, reserving the thickened liquid. Discard the seeds and fibres left in the sieve.

Rinse the rice and cook in boiling, lightly salted water for about 12 minutes until just tender. Drain thoroughly and pour a cupful of cold water through it to cool it. Drain, and put into a large bowl.

Heat the oil in a frying pan, add all the seeds and fry gently for 2 minutes. Add the almonds and fry until golden. Add the contents of the pan to the rice with the tamarind liquid, chillies and chopped coriander leaves. Stir together lightly and season to taste.

MANGO RICE
Serves 6

350 g/12 oz basmati rice
salt
½ teaspoon turmeric
1 large ripe mango
2 tablespoons oil
2 tablespoons lime or lemon juice
freshly ground black pepper
50 g/2 oz cashew nuts

Rinse the rice and cook in boiling, lightly salted water with the turmeric, for about 12 minutes until tender. Drain thoroughly and pour a cupful of cold water through it to cool it. Drain and put into a salad bowl. Peel the mango. Grate the flesh away from the large central stone onto a plate to catch the juice. Add to the rice with the oil and lime or lemon juice. Toss lightly together and season to taste. Scatter the cashew nuts over the top just before serving.

BROWN RICE SALAD
Serves 6

350 g/12 oz long grain brown rice
2 courgettes, finely chopped
salt
1 red pepper, seeded and chopped
2 tablespoons chopped parsley
½ teaspoon dried oregano
5 tablespoons olive oil
3 tablespoons lemon juice
1 clove garlic, crushed
freshly ground black pepper

Rinse the rice and cook in boiling, lightly salted water for about 35 minutes until tender. Drain. Rinse with cold water and drain thoroughly. Put into a salad bowl. Add the courgettes, red pepper and herbs. Mix the oil, lemon juice and garlic. Pour over the salad, season and toss together gently.

GINGERED CHINESE SALAD
Serves 6

3 tablespoons oil
2 carrots, sliced diagonally
2.5-cm/1-inch piece fresh root ginger, grated
1 garlic clove, crushed
2 tablespoons soy sauce
1 tablespoon sherry
½ head of Chinese leaves, shredded
225-g/9-oz can sliced bamboo shoots, drained
salt and freshly ground black pepper

Heat the oil in a wok or large frying pan, add the carrot and stir-fry for 1 minute. Add the ginger and garlic and fry for a further 2 minutes. Add the soy sauce and sherry; tip into a heatproof salad bowl. Add the Chinese leaves and bamboo shoots and toss together lightly. Season to taste.

CELERY, MUSHROOM AND BANANA
Serves 6

6 sticks celery, thickly sliced
350 g/12 oz button mushrooms, thickly sliced
150 ml/¼ pint natural yogurt
4 tablespoons mayonnaise
2 ripe bananas
1 tablespoon lemon juice
salt and freshly ground black pepper

Put the celery, mushrooms and yogurt into a salad bowl, mix together and allow to marinate for 30 minutes. Add mayonnaise. Slice the bananas into the lemon juice to prevent them from going brown; then add them to the salad with plenty of seasoning. Toss gently and serve within 1 hour.

RUSSIAN SALAD
Serves 6

3 large waxy potatoes, peeled and diced
3 large carrots, peeled and diced
salt and freshly ground black pepper
225 g/8 oz French beans, topped and tailed
100 g/4 oz frozen peas
1 quantity of Basic Mayonnaise (see page 18)
1 teaspoon mild mustard

Cook the potatoes and carrots together in boiling, lightly salted water for about 5 minutes or until just tender. Cut beans into 2.5-cm/1-inch lengths. Steam the beans and peas in a colander over the pan of potatoes for 3 minutes. Drain vegetables thoroughly and put into a salad bowl. Allow to cool. Stir in the mayonnaise and mustard and season to taste.

TABBOULEH
Serves 6

225 g/8 oz fine cracked wheat (also called burghul or pourgouri)
6 spring onions, finely chopped
1 teaspoon dried mint
6 tablespoons chopped parsley
1 cucumber, finely chopped
3 tomatoes, finely chopped
3 tablespoons lemon juice
2 tablespoons olive oil
cos lettuce heart

Rinse the cracked wheat with cold water until the water runs clear. Drain thoroughly and place in a large bowl. Add the spring onions, chopped herbs and vegetables. Stir together well. Mix the lemon juice and oil and pour over the salad. Toss well to make sure everything is evenly coated with the dressing. Serve piled on a serving platter, surrounded by cos lettuce leaves. Use the leaves, if you wish, to scoop up the salad.

HOT PASTA WITH BROCCOLI
Serves 6

**350 g/12 oz mixed green and white ribbon
   noodles**
salt
225 g/8 oz broccoli
**1 quantity of Vinaigrette Dressing
   (see page 16)**
4 tablespoons grated Parmesan cheese
12 small black olives
freshly ground black pepper

Cook the pasta in boiling, lightly salted water until
just tender. Meanwhile divide the broccoli into
florets and steam for 4 minutes in a colander over a
pan of boiling water until tender. Drain pasta
thoroughly and put into a large heatproof bowl with
the broccoli. Add the vinaigrette dressing, Parmesan
cheese and olives. Toss together lightly and add
plenty of black pepper. Serve immediately.

HOT BUTTONS AND BOWS
Serves 6

350 g/12 oz pasta bows
salt
4 tablespoons oil
25 g/1 oz butter
350 g/12 oz small button mushrooms, trimmed
2 cloves garlic, crushed
4 tablespoons chopped parsley
freshly ground black pepper
rind of 1 lemon

Cook the pasta in boiling, lightly salted water until
just tender. Meanwhile heat the oil and butter in a
frying pan, add the mushrooms and fry for 3
minutes. Add garlic, half the parsley and seasoning
and cook for a further 2 minutes. Cut strips of rind
from the lemon with a potato peeler. Chop it roughly
and mix it with the remaining parsley. Drain the
pasta thoroughly and put into a heatproof salad bowl.
Pour the mushrooms and juices over the pasta and
toss lightly together. Sprinkle the lemon and parsley
mixture over the salad and serve immediately.

SPAGHETTI WITH ARTICHOKES
Serves 6

4 large tomatoes, peeled
397-g/14-oz can artichoke hearts, drained
1 tablespoon chopped parsley
**1 quantity of Vinaigrette Dressing
   (see page 16)**
3 or 4 drops Tabasco sauce
350 g/12 oz spaghetti
salt and finely ground black pepper

Cut the tomatoes into wedges, discarding seeds. Put
into a large salad bowl. Quarter the artichoke hearts
and add, with the parsley and dressing, to the bowl.
Add Tabasco sauce, stir together lightly and allow to
stand for 1 hour to allow the flavours to mingle.
Break the spaghetti into 7.5-cm/3-inch lengths and
cook in boiling, lightly salted water until just tender.
Drain and pour a cupful of cold water through it to
cool it slightly. Drain thoroughly before adding to
the salad bowl. Toss gently and season to taste with
lots of black pepper. Serve immediately.

CRUNCHY PASTA SALAD
Serves 6

350 g/12 oz pasta spirals
salt
225 g/8 oz French beans, topped and tailed
1 avocado, peeled and cut into cubes
2 dessert apples, cored and chopped
2 tablespoons lemon juice
1 quantity of Basic Mayonnaise (see page 18)
freshly ground black pepper

Cook the pasta in boiling, lightly salted water until
just tender. Steam the beans in a colander over the
pasta for 5 minutes. Drain pasta and rinse with the
beans under cold water. Drain thoroughly and put
into a salad bowl. In a separate bowl toss the avocado
and apples in the lemon juice. Add, with the
mayonnaise, to the pasta. Toss together gently until
evenly coated. Season to taste.

TRAFFIC LIGHT PEPPERS
Serves 4 to 6

1 small green pepper, seeded and sliced
1 small red pepper, seeded and sliced
1 small yellow pepper, seeded and sliced
1 mild Spanish onion, thinly sliced
1 quantity of Vinaigrette Dressing
  (see page 16)
1 teaspoon sugar
chopped parsley, to garnish

Put the sliced peppers into a bowl and stir together to mix the colours. Divide the onion slices into rings and add to the peppers. Mix the dressing and sugar, pour over the vegetables and toss together. Leave for 2 hours before serving to allow the salad to soften. Sprinkle with chopped parsley before serving.

SPICED CAULIFLOWER
Serves 6

This salad is delicious hot or cold with chicken or ham. It's best made the day before serving so that the flavour mellows.

5 tablespoons oil
1 onion, thinly sliced
2 teaspoons mild curry paste
½ teaspoon turmeric
1 large cauliflower, divided into florets
2 teaspoons yellow mustard seeds
6 tablespoons water
salt and freshly ground black pepper

Heat the oil in a saucepan or flameproof casserole. Add the onion and fry gently until transparent. Stir in the curry paste and turmeric. Add the cauliflower and mustard seeds and fry, stirring occasionally, for 2

minutes. Add the water. Cover, reduce the heat and cook for 5 minutes until the cauliflower is just tender. Season to taste and serve warm or cold.

KOHLRABI WITH GREEN MAYONNAISE
Serves 6

4 kohlrabi, about 550 g/1¼ lb, peeled
salt
4 tablespoons mayonnaise
4 tablespoons natural yogurt
1 tablespoon chopped parsley
1 tablespoon chopped chives
1 tablespoon chopped spring onion
freshly ground black pepper
2 hard-boiled eggs, shelled and chopped

Peel the kohlrabi and cut into thick slices. Cut each slice into quarters. Blanch in boiling, lightly salted water for 1 minute. Rinse under cold water and drain thoroughly. Put into a large bowl with the mayonnaise, yogurt, herbs and spring onion. Toss together lightly and season to taste. Stir in the chopped hard-boiled eggs.

CELERIAC RÉMOULADE
Serves 6

1 large celeriac root, peeled and cut into
   matchsticks
4 tablespoons vinegar
6 tablespoons mayonnaise
1 tablespoon Dijon mustard
salt and freshly ground black pepper

As you cut the celeriac matchsticks, put them immediately into a bowl of cold water with half the vinegar. This stops them turning brown. Add the remaining vinegar to a saucepan of water and bring to the boil. Add the drained celeriac and bring back to the boil. Tip into a colander and rinse with cold water. Drain thoroughly and put into a large bowl. Mix the mayonnaise, mustard, salt and pepper together and add to the celeriac. Mix together and set aside for 2 hours to allow the flavours to develop.
Transfer to a serving dish.

ADUKI BEANS WITH BACON AND PINEAPLLE
Serves 6

225 g/8 oz dried aduki beans
100 g/4 oz basmati rice
425-g/15-oz can pineapple pieces in natural
   juice
6 tablespoons oil
175 g/6 oz rindless smoked streaky bacon
salt and freshly ground black pepper

Rinse the beans, put into a large saucepan and cover with plenty of cold water. Bring to the boil and boil for 2 minutes. Remove from the heat, cover and leave to soak for 1 hour. Drain and rinse, cover with fresh water and again bring to the boil. Boil rapidly for 10 minutes, then simmer for about 50 minutes until tender. Meanwhile, wash rice and cook in boiling, lightly salted water for 15 minutes until tender. Drain, rinse with cold water and put into a salad bowl. Add the canned pineapple pieces with 4 tablespoons of the juice, and the oil. Drain the beans; stir into the rice. Leave to cool slightly. Grill the bacon until crisp and golden, snip into strips and add to the salad. Toss together lightly and season to taste.

RED BEANS WITH SWEET CORN
Serves 6

175 g/6 oz dried red kidney beans
225 g/8 oz French beans, topped and tailed
225 g/8 oz frozen sweet corn kernels
1 quantity of Vinaigrette Dressing
   (see page 16)
1 teaspoon honey
1 tablespoon chopped parsley
salt and freshly ground black pepper

Rinse the beans, put into a large saucepan and cover with plenty of cold water. Bring to the boil and boil for 2 minutes. Remove from the heat, cover and leave to soak for 1 hour. Drain and rinse the beans thoroughly, return to the pan, cover with fresh water and again bring to the boil. Boil rapidly for 10 minutes, then simmer for about 1 hour until tender. Meanwhile, cut the French beans into 2.5-cm/1-inch lengths and steam with the corn in a colander over a pan of boiling water for 3 minutes. Put into a salad bowl with the dressing and honey. Drain the kidney beans and add to the bowl. Toss together lightly and leave to cool. Add parsley and salt and pepper to taste. Toss and serve.

BUTTER BEANS WITH ANCHOVIES
Serves 6

225 g/8 oz dried butter beans
1 small onion, finely chopped
2 tablespoons chopped savory or parsley
6 tablespoons oil
2 tablespoons lemon juice
50-g/2-oz can anchovy fillets in oil
freshly ground black pepper

Rinse the beans, put in a pan and cover with cold water. Bring to the boil and boil for 2 minutes. Remove from the heat, cover and leave to soak for 1 hour. Rinse, cover with fresh cold water and boil again for 10 minutes. Simmer for about 50 minutes until just tender. Meanwhile, put onion, savory or parsley, oil and lemon juice into a heatproof bowl and leave to marinate. Drain beans thoroughly and add to dressing. Add oil from can of anchovies and anchovy fillets snipped into pieces. Grind lots of black pepper over the salad and toss together. Serve slightly warm or cold.

HARICOT BEANS WITH TOMATOES
Serves 6

350 g/12 oz dried haricot beans
2 large onions, chopped
6 tablespoons oil
2 cloves garlic, crushed
397-g/14-oz can tomatoes
3 tablespoons tomato purée
1 tablespoon paprika
salt and freshly ground black pepper
flat-leafed parsley

Rinse the beans, put into a saucepan, and cover with plenty of cold water. Bring to the boil and boil for 2 minutes. Remove from the heat, cover and leave to soak for 1 hour. Rinse, cover with fresh water and boil again for 10 minutes. Simmer for 50 minutes. Meanwhile, heat the oil in a large pan and fry the onions until transparent. Add the garlic, tomatoes and juice, and tomato purée. Drain the beans, reserving 300 ml/½ pint of the cooking liquid. Add beans, reserved liquid, paprika and seasoning to the tomatoes. Simmer uncovered for about 20 minutes, until beans are tender and the liquid is reduced to a sauce. Allow to cool. Scatter snipped parsley over the salad before serving.

WHEAT SPROUTS WITH APPLE AND CELERY
Serves 6

175 g/6 oz wheat sprouts
2 dessert apples, cored and diced
1 tablespoon lemon juice
4 sticks celery, sliced
2 tablespoons oil
salt and freshly ground black pepper
1 teaspoon poppy seeds

Pick over the grain sprouts, discarding any grains that have not sprouted. Put into a salad bowl. Toss the diced apple in the lemon juice to prevent it browning. Add to the sprouts with the celery and oil. Season and toss together lightly. Sprinkle the poppy seeds over the salad and serve immediately.

GREEN BEAN SPROUT SALAD
Serves 6

225 g/8 oz sprouted flageolet beans
1 small iceberg lettuce, shredded
100 g/4 oz curly kale, finely chopped
1 small head of chicory, shredded
5 tablespoons oil
1 tablespoon lemon juice
salt and freshly ground black pepper
1 tablespoon snipped chives

Pick over the sprouts, discarding loose husks, and any beans that have not sprouted. Put into a salad bowl with the shredded lettuce, kale and chicory. Add the oil and lemon juice, season and toss together lightly. Sprinkle the chives over the salad and serve immediately.

ALFALFA WITH SWEET AND SOUR CARROTS
Serves 6

3 medium-sized carrots
1 small red onion, thinly sliced
150 ml/¼ pint white wine vinegar
1 tablespoon sugar
1 teaspoon coriander seeds
100 g/4 oz alfalfa sprouts
2 tablespoons oil
salt and freshly ground black pepper

Cut the carrots into matchsticks; put into a heatproof bowl with the onion. Put the vinegar, sugar and coriander seeds into a saucepan and bring to the boil. Pour over the carrots and allow to cool. Pick over the alfalfa sprouts and put into a salad bowl. Drain the carrot mixture, discarding the vinegar. Add to the sprouts with the oil and seasoning and toss together lightly. Serve immediately.

BEAN SPROUTS WITH HAZELNUT DRESSING
Serves 6

225 g/8 oz mung bean sprouts
1 bunch watercress
1 green pepper, seeded and sliced
25 g/1 oz toasted hazelnuts
6 tablespoons oil
2 teaspoons white wine vinegar
salt and freshly ground black pepper

Pick over the bean sprouts, discarding any loose husks. Put into a large salad bowl. Tear the watercress into manageable pieces; add to the sprouts with the green pepper. Grind the nuts in a liquidiser, gradually adding the oil and vinegar. Season the dressing well and pour over the salad. Toss together lightly and serve immediately.

RED CABBAGE AND APPLE WITH CREAM CHEESE DRESSING
Serves 6

450 g/1 lb red cabbage, finely shredded
2 crisp eating apples, quartered, cored and
  sliced
1 teaspoon caraway seeds
75 g/3 oz cream cheese
6 tablespoons single cream
salt and freshly ground black pepper

Put the shredded red cabbage into a large bowl with the sliced apples and caraway seeds. Mix the cream cheese with the cream to make a smooth dressing. Season and pour over the salad. Toss well and leave for about 1 hour to allow the cabbage to soften slightly before serving.

CAULIFLOWER WITH GARLIC CREAM
Serves 6

1 medium-sized green cauliflower
1 small cauliflower
1 clove garlic, crushed
1 tablespoon white wine vinegar
150 ml/¼ pint single cream
salt and freshly ground black pepper
50 g/2 oz Italian salami, thinly sliced

Cut the green and white cauliflower into florets of even size. Steam together in a colander over a saucepan of boiling water for 5 minutes, turning once or twice. Arrange on a serving dish and allow to cool slightly. Mix the garlic, vinegar and cream together and season to taste. Spoon over the cauliflower. Cut the salami into fine strips and scatter over the salad. Serve slightly warm.

BROAD BEANS WITH TOMATOES AND HERBS
Serves 6

450 g/1 lb fresh or frozen broad beans
salt
225 g/8 oz cherry tomatoes, quartered
5 tablespoons oil
1 tablespoon red wine vinegar
1 tablespoon chopped parsley
1 tablespoon chopped tarragon
freshly ground black pepper

Cook the beans in boiling, lightly salted water for about 10 minutes until tender. Drain and rinse with cold water. Put into a salad bowl with the tomatoes, oil, vinegar and herbs. Season and toss together.

RED AND WHITE RADISH WITH CUCUMBER
Serves 6

1 bunch red radishes, trimmed and sliced
1 mooli or daikon radish, trimmed and sliced
1 cucumber, sliced
2 tablespoons oil
1 teaspoon white wine vinegar
¼ teaspoon sugar
salt and freshly ground black pepper
1 teaspoon chopped fresh dill

Put the radish and cucumber slices in a salad bowl with the oil, vinegar, sugar and seasoning. Toss together lightly. Sprinkle the dill over the salad.

MAIN DISH SALADS

SPICED CHICKEN WITH APRICOTS
Serves 6

1 tablespoon oil
1 large onion, finely chopped
1 tablespoon curry paste
1 tablespoon coriander seeds, crushed
2 tablespoons lemon juice
150 ml/ ¼ pint thick mayonnaise
150 ml/ ¼ pint natural yogurt
425-g/15-oz can apricot halves in fruit juice
450 g/1 lb boneless cooked chicken, neatly
   sliced
salt and freshly ground black pepper
½ Webb's lettuce
2 tablespoons desiccated coconut, toasted

Heat the oil in a small pan and fry the onion until transparent. Add the curry paste and coriander; fry gently for 2 minutes. Add the lemon juice and allow to cool. Put into a bowl with the mayonnaise and yogurt. Drain and quarter the apricots; stir into the mayonnaise with the chicken. Toss together gently. Season to taste. Separate the chicory leaves and arrange round the edge of a large serving platter. Pile the salad in the centre and top with the coconut. Serve immediately.

PEARS, CHICORY AND WALNUT CHEESE
Serves 6

4 firm dessert pears
1 head of chicory
½ iceberg lettuce, shredded
4 tablespoons oil
1 tablespoon lemon juice
1 teaspoon chopped fresh tarragon
salt and freshly ground black pepper
350 g/12 oz Red Leicester with Walnuts

Quarter the pears and remove the core. Cut the pears into thin slices. Separate the chicory leaves, and cut across into 2.5-cm/1-inch slices. Put the chicory into a salad bowl with the lettuce, pears, oil, lemon juice and tarragon. Season to taste. Cut the cheese into small cubes, add to the salad and toss together lightly.

SEAFOOD SALAD
Serves 6

1 kg/2.2 lb fresh mussels
6 tablespoons white wine
225 g/8 oz peeled prawns
350 g/12 oz cleaned squid, cut into rings
2 tablespoons vinegar
2 large carrots, cut into matchsticks
¼ small white cabbage, finely shredded
150 ml/¼ pint olive oil
1 clove garlic, crushed
2 tablespoons lemon juice
salt and freshly ground black pepper

Scrub the mussels in cold water; discard any that are open. Put them in a saucepan with the white wine. Cover and cook on a high heat for 5 minutes or until the shells are open. Allow to cool; then remove mussels from their shells. Put them into a bowl with the prawns. Poach the squid in gently simmering water and the vinegar for 5 minutes. Drain and cool. Add to the bowl with the carrot and cabbage. Pour the oil, garlic and lemon juice over the mixture. Season. Allow to marinate for 3 to 4 hours before serving with crusty bread.

SALT BEEF SALAD
Serves 6

225 g/8 oz tiny pickling (button) onions
6 tablespoons olive oil
1 tablespoon white wine vinegar
2 teaspoons Dijon mustard
salt and freshly ground black pepper
350 g/12 oz young, tender spinach leaves
350 g/12 oz sliced salt beef
2 dill-pickled cucumbers, sliced

Soak the onions in hot water for 10 minutes to loosen the skins. Peel the onions and blanch in boiling water for 5 minutes. Drain thoroughly. Put the oil, vinegar, mustard and seasoning into a salad bowl. Add the onions and spinach leaves and toss together. Cut the salt beef into strips; stir into the salad with the dill cucumber. Serve with rye bread and butter.

MIXED GREENS WITH GOAT'S CHEESE
Serves 6

6 cos lettuce leaves
handful of oak leaf lettuce
handful of curly endive
5 tablespoons oil
1 tablespoon white wine vinegar
1 teaspoon dried mustard
salt and freshly ground black pepper
¼ small red cabbage, finely shredded
225 g/8 oz goat's cheese
100 g/4 oz curd cheese
6 thick slices wholemeal bread

Tear all the lettuce and the curly endive into manageable pieces. Mix the oil, vinegar, mustard and seasoning in a large bowl. Add the leaves and cabbage and toss until evenly coated. Divide salad between individual plates. Mash the goat's cheese and curd

cheese together. Toast the bread lightly on both sides. Cut off the crusts. Spread the cheese over one side and grill for 1 minute until warm. Cut each piece into four. Serve the goat cheese croutons on the salad while still warm.

SALAD NIÇOISE
Serves 6

225 g/8 oz French beans, topped and tailed
2 198-g/7-oz cans tuna in brine, drained
350 g/12 oz small firm tomatoes, quartered
1 shallot, thinly sliced
50 g/2 oz small black olives
6 cos lettuce leaves
1 quantity of Vinaigrette Dressing
  (see page 16)
3 hard–boiled eggs

Steam the beans in a colander over a pan of boiling water for 5 minutes until tender. Flake the tuna and put into a salad bowl with the tomatoes, shallot and olives. Tear the lettuce into manageable pieces. Add to the salad with the beans and vinaigrette dressing, and toss together lightly. Quarter the hard-boiled eggs and stir in gently. Serve immediately with large floury baps.

SWORDFISH SALAD
Serves 6

This unusual Mediterranean fish in now a fairly common sight in supermarkets and good fish shops. If you can't find it, use thick cod steaks or monk fish instead.

675 g/1½ lb swordfish steaks
1 bay leaf
1 small onion, quartered
½ lemon, sliced
675 g/1½ lb leeks, trimmed
salt and freshly ground black pepper
4 tablespoons dry white vermouth
2 egg yolks
pinch of cayenne
1 tablespoon lemon juice
200-g/7-oz can red pimientoes
6 small black olives

Put the swordfish steaks in a frying pan with 450 ml/¾ pint water to half cover them. Add the bay leaf, onion and lemon slices. Bring to simmering point, cover and poach for about 10 minutes until the fish flakes easily when tested with a knife. Leave to cool in the liquid. Slice the leeks thinly and separate into rings. Steam in a colander over a pan of boiling water for 3 minutes. Season and arrange on a large flat dish. Lift the fish steaks out of the liquid. Flake and reserve fish, discarding skin and bones. Boil the fish stock rapidly until reduced to one quarter; then add the vermouth. Put the egg yolks, cayenne and lemon juice into a bowl over a pan of hot water and beat well together. Gradually add the fish stock, beating constantly until thickened. Stir in the flaked fish. Spoon on top of the shredded leeks. Cut the red pimiento into strips. Arrange the pimiento and the black olives on the fish before serving.

ORIENTAL TURKEY
Serves 6

350 g/12 oz spring greens
oil for frying
4 fresh or canned baby sweet corn cobs
225 g/8 oz bean sprouts
1 teaspoon oil
1 teaspoon soy sauce
1 tablespoon sesame seeds, toasted
½ teaspoon sugar
175 g/6 oz sliced smoked turkey or ham

Trim the spring greens, discarding tough stalks. Shred finely. Heat 2.5 cm/1 inch oil in a saucepan. Add the shredded greens a handful at a time and fry for about 1 minute until crisp and golden. Lift out and drain on absorbent kitchen paper. Cut corn cobs diagonally into thin slices. Steam in a colander over boiling water for 2 minutes until just tender. Put into a bowl with the bean sprouts, oil, soy sauce, sesame seeds and sugar. Cut the turkey into fine strips and add to the salad with the spring greens. Toss together lightly before serving.

CHUNKY CHEESE SALAD
Serves 6

½ small white cabbage, shredded
½ small red cabbage, shredded
100 g/4 oz carrots, peeled and grated
1 small cauliflower, cut into small florets
½ cucumber, chopped
225 g/8 oz tomatoes, chopped
100 g/4 oz button mushrooms, sliced
5 tablespoons oil
1 tablespoon vinegar
75 g/3 oz salted peanuts
175 g/6 oz Red Leicester cheese, grated
100 g/4 oz Lancashire cheese, grated

Put the red and white cabbage into a large bowl with the carrots, cauliflower, cucumber, tomatoes and mushrooms. Add the oil and vinegar and toss together. Leave for 1 hour to soften slightly. Just before serving add the peanuts and grated cheese. Toss together lightly. Serve with wholemeal bread.

CUCUMBER WITH SMOKED MACKEREL
Serves 6

1 cucumber
1 small onion, thinly sliced
4 tablespoons white wine vinegar
1 teaspoon sugar
1 round lettuce
handful of oak leaf lettuce
2 tablespoons oil
450 g/1 lb peppered smoked mackerel fillets

Cut cucumber in half lengthways and scoop out the seeds with a teaspoon. Slice thinly. Put into a salad bowl with the onion, vinegar and sugar. Leave to marinate for 30 minutes. Tear the round and oak leaf lettuce into manageable pieces. Add the oil to the cucumber mixture. Add the lettuce leaves and toss together lightly. Flake the mackerel, discarding any bones and skin. Add to the salad and mix gently. Serve with crusty Granary bread and butter.

PENNE WITH ST PAULIN CHEESE
Serves 6

You will find this mild soft cheese with the distinctive orange rind in the chill cabinet of your supermarket. The hot pasta melts it slightly to give a creamy texture to this interesting hot/cold salad.

350 g/12 oz penne nib-shaped pasta
salt
450 g/1 lb plum tomatoes
5 tablespoons olive oil
6 fresh basil leaves
350 g/12 oz St Paulin cheese
freshly ground black pepper

Cook the pasta in boiling, lightly salted water until just tender. Meanwhile, quarter the tomatoes and discard the seeds. Chop the tomatoes finely. Put into a heatproof bowl with the oil and snipped basil. Cut off the orange-coloured rind and cut the cheese into tiny cubes. Add to the tomatoes. Season, adding plenty of black pepper. Drain the pasta thoroughly and add to the tomatoes. Toss well and serve immediately while still warm.

CHEF'S SALAD
Serves 6

25 g/1 oz walnuts, chopped
50 g/2 oz sultanas
3 sticks celery, sliced
1 green pepper, seeded and chopped
2 red-skinned apples, cored and chopped
2 tablespoons mayonnaise
3 tablespoons single cream
1 teaspoon lemon juice
salt and freshly ground black pepper
1 small iceberg lettuce
225 g/8 oz Caerphilly cheese, cubed
2 1-cm/½-inch thick slices of ham, cubed

Put the walnuts, sultanas, celery, pepper and apples together in a large bowl. Add the mayonnaise, cream, lemon juice and seasonings; toss well until evenly coated. Separate the lettuce leaves and use some to line a salad bowl. Tear the rest into pieces and toss with the salad. Pile the salad inside the lettuce leaves. Scatter the cubes of cheese and ham over. Stir into the salad just before serving.

GREEK SALAD
Serves 6

6 tablespoons olive oil
2 tablespoons lemon juice
1 tablespoon chopped fresh mint
½ teaspoon dried oregano
salt and freshly ground black pepper
1 cos lettuce, torn into manageable pieces
100 g/4 oz white cabbage, finely shredded
½ cucumber, halved and sliced
6 small firm tomatoes, cut into wedges
12 small black olives
350 g/12 oz feta cheese

Beat the oil, lemon juice, mint, oregano and seasoning together in a salad bowl. Add the lettuce, cabbage, cucumber, tomatoes and olives. Toss together lightly. Drain the feta cheese and cut into small cubes. Stir gently into the salad. Serve with hot pitta bread.

STROGANOFF SALAD
Serves 6

225 g/8 oz green ribbon noodles
salt
350 g/12 oz thickly sliced cold roast beef
350 g/12 oz button mushrooms, thickly sliced
6 spring onions, thinly sliced
300 ml/½ pint soured cream
1 tablespoon coarse-grained mustard
freshly ground black pepper

Cook the noodles in boiling, lightly salted water until just tender. Drain, rinse with cold water and drain again thoroughly. Put into a salad bowl. Cut the beef into strips and add to the pasta with the mushrooms and spring onions. Add the cream, mustard and seasoning and toss together lightly. Leave for an hour or so before serving to allow the flavours to mingle.

CEVICHE
Serves 6

Be sure to buy fresh fish for this uncooked salad.

450 g/1 lb fresh monkfish fillet
225 g/8 oz fresh pink trout fillets, skinned
juice of 2 limes
juice of 1 lemon
1 fresh green chilli, thinly sliced
4 tablespoons olive oil
salt and freshly ground black pepper
2 beefsteak tomatoes, thinly sliced
few sprigs flat-leafed parsley

Cut the monkfish and trout fillets into neat
2.5-cm/1-inch pieces. Put into a glass bowl and add
the lime juice, lemon juice and chilli. Leave to
marinate for 6 to 8 hours, stirring occasionally until
the fish becomes opaque and has a cooked appearance. Add the oil and season to taste. Arrange the
tomato slices on a shallow serving dish, pile the fish
mixture in the centre. Scatter the
snipped parsley over the top.

PASTA AND TUNA
Serves 6

350 g/12 oz pasta shells
salt
198-g/7-oz can tuna in oil
1 small onion, finely chopped
½ cucumber, roughly chopped
5 tablespoons mayonnaise
3 tablespoons natural yogurt
grated rind and juice of 1 lemon
freshly ground black pepper
lettuce leaves to garnish

Cook the pasta in boiling, lightly salted water until tender. Drain and rinse with cold water. Put into a large bowl. Add the tuna and its oil, breaking the fish into pieces. Add the onion, cucumber, mayonnaise, yogurt, lemon rind and lemon juice. Toss gently until the pasta is evenly coated. Season to taste. Arrange the lettuce leaves around the edge of a large serving dish. Pile the pasta salad in the centre.

SHREDDED OMELETTE SALAD

Serves 6

1 red pepper, seeded
1 teaspoon tomato purée
12 eggs
salt and freshly ground black pepper
3 teaspoons oil
1 yellow pepper, seeded
4 tablespoons chopped parsley
2 tablespoons Parmesan, grated
225 g/8 oz cherry tomatoes, thinly sliced

Finely chop the red pepper. Put into a bowl with the tomato purée, four of the eggs and seasoning. Heat a teaspoon of the oil in a large non-stick frying pan, add the egg mixture, tipping the pan to cover the base. Cook until lightly set. Slide the omelette out of the pan onto a board. Chop the yellow pepper, add to four more beaten eggs. Season and make another omelette in the same way. Tip out of the pan. Add parsley and Parmesan to the last four eggs and make another omelette. Roll up each omelette and slice neatly. Mix all the omelettes in a large salad bowl. Add the sliced tomatoes and toss lightly together. Season to taste.

ROAST DUCK SALAD

Serves 6

1 oven-ready duckling, thawed if frozen
salt and freshly ground black pepper
225 g/8 oz frozen petits pois
5 tablespoons oil
3 tablespoons orange juice
1 teaspoon honey
1 cos lettuce heart
1 bunch watercress, trimmed
2 shallots, thinly sliced

Prick the duck all over the breast. Rub a little salt into the skin. Place the duck on a rack in a roasting tin and cook at 200°C/400°F/Gas 6 for 30 minutes per 450 g/1 lb or until the juices run clear when the thickest meat is pierced with a fine skewer. Meanwhile, steam the peas in a colander over boiling water for 2 minutes. Cool. Remove all the crispy skin from the breast of the duck and reserve. Leave the duck and skin to cool. Put the oil, orange juice, honey and seasoning into a salad bowl. Put in the crossed salad servers. Tear the lettuce into manageable pieces. Pile the lettuce leaves and watercress on top. Cut meat off the duck and cut into neat pieces. Add to the salad with shallots and peas. Toss together lightly. Snip pieces of duck skin into strips and scatter over the salad just before serving.

INDEX